THE JOY OF
ELGAR

D11980948X0100

WISE PUBLICATIONS
part of The Music Sales Group

London / New York / Paris / Sydney / Copenhagen / Berlin / Hong Kong / Tokyo / Madrid

Published by
Wise Publications
14-15 Berners Street, London W1T 3LJ, UK.

Exclusive Distributors:
Music Sales Limited
Distribution Centre, Newmarket Road, Bury St. Edmunds, Suffolk IP33 3YB, UK.
Music Sales Corporation
Music Sales Corporation, 180 Madison Avenue, 24th Floor, New York NY 10016, USA.
Music Sales Pty Limited
Music Sales Pty., Units 3-4, 17 Willfox Street, Condell Park, NSW 2200, Australia.

Order No. AM1008810
ISBN: 978-1-78305-538-8
This book © Copyright 2014 Wise Publications,
a division of Music Sales Limited.

Edited by Sam Lung.
Arrangements by Camden Music Services.
Music engraved by Camden Music Services and Elius Gravure Musicale.
Cover designed by Tim Field.

Printed in the EU.

Cello Concerto in E Minor, Op.85

1st Movement

Edward Elgar

Chanson de Matin, Op.15 No.2

Edward Elgar

Cockaigne (In London Town), Op.40

'Cockaigne Overture'

Edward Elgar

Contrasts: The Gavotte A.D. 1700 and 1900

from Three Characteristic Pieces, Op.10

Edward Elgar

con Ped.

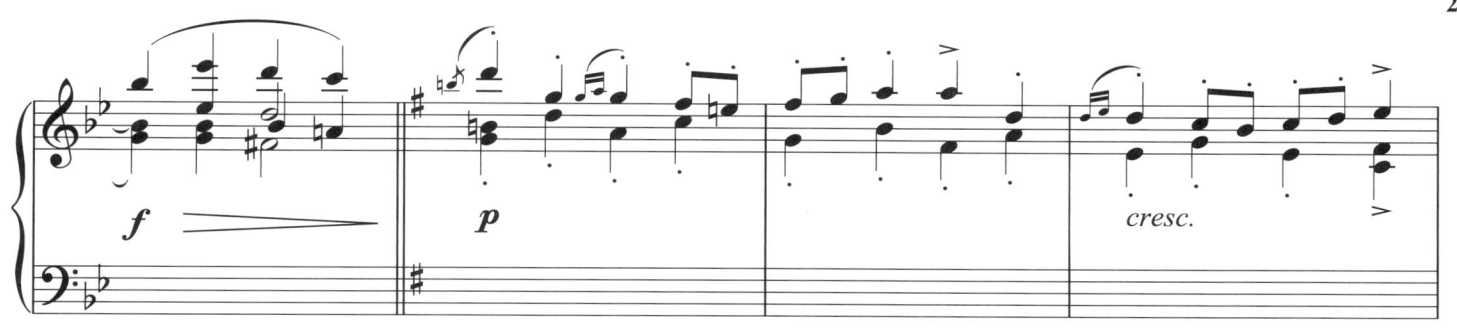

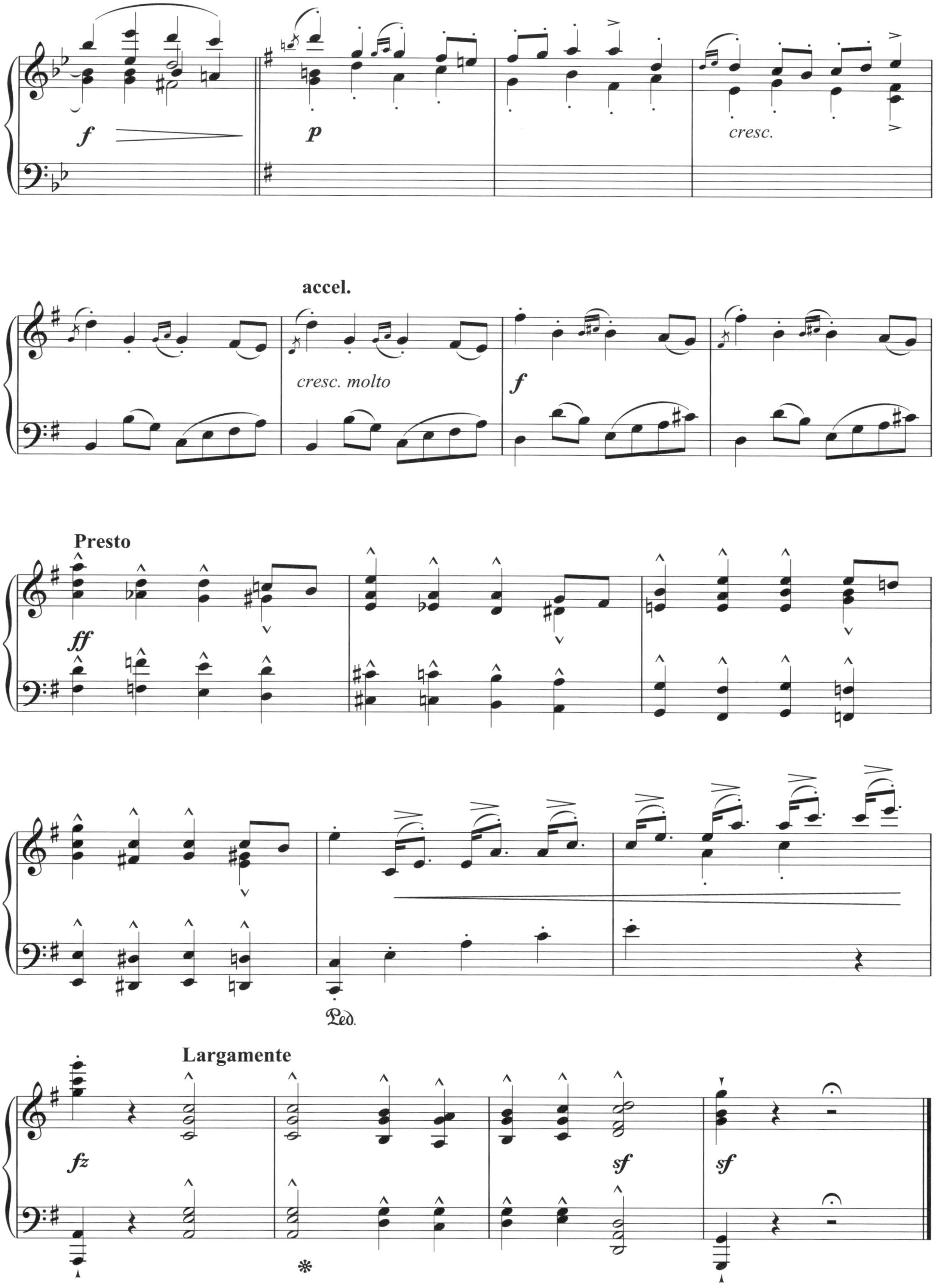
f
p
cresc.
accel.
cresc. molto
f
Presto
ff
Ped.
Largamente
fz
sf
sf

Interlude No.1

'Jack Falstaff, page to the Duke of Norfolk.'

from Falstaff, Op.68

Edward Elgar

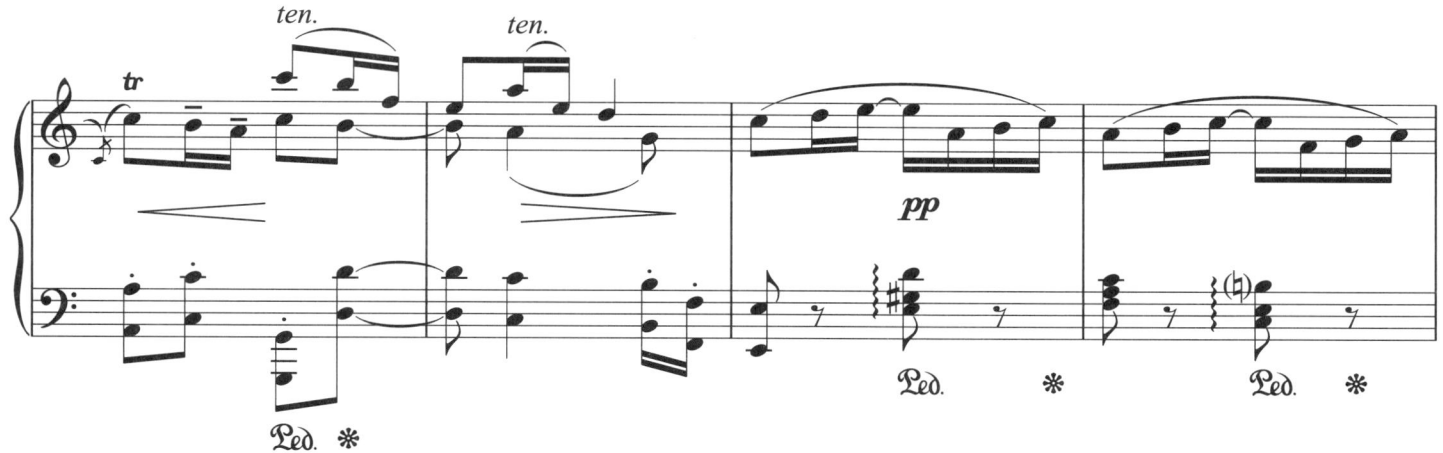

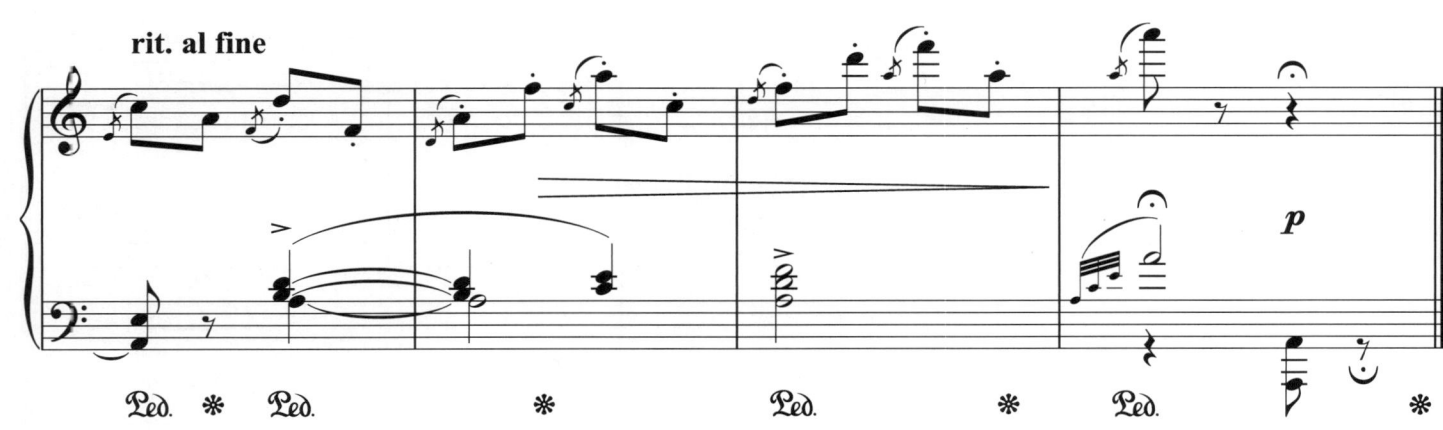

Interlude No.2

Gloucestershire; Shallow's Orchard.

from Falstaff, Op.68

Edward Elgar

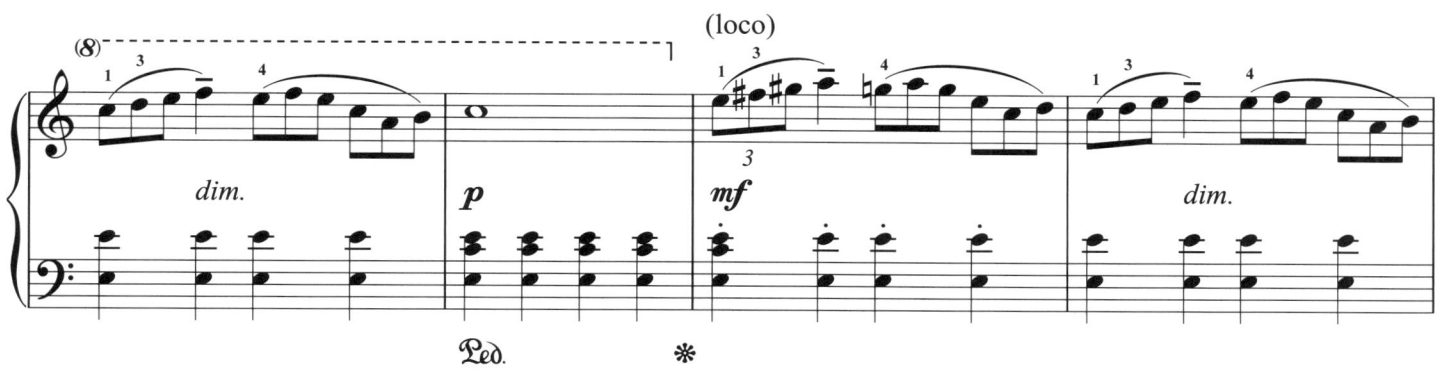

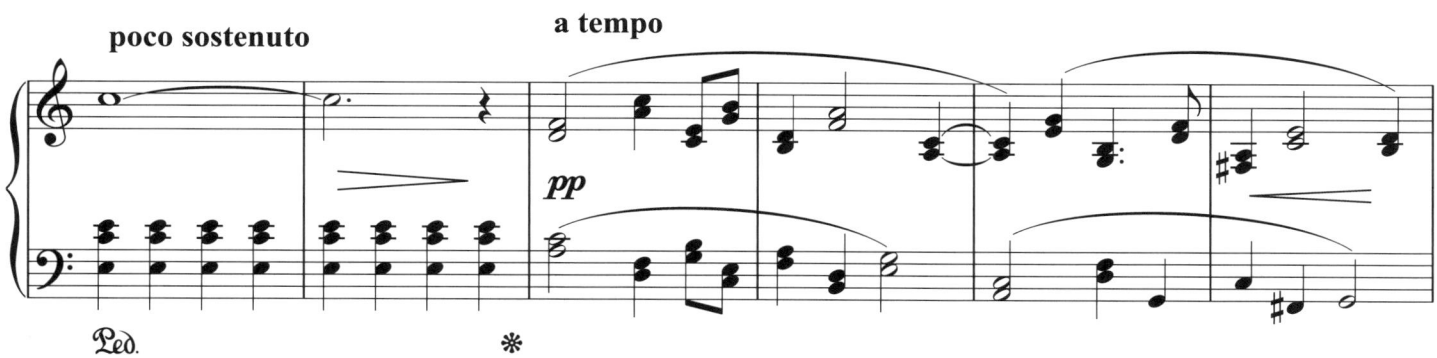

Pomp & Circumstance March No.1, Op.39

Edward Elgar

(animato)

TRIO
Largamente

Molto maestoso

allargando

a tempo

Mazurka

from Three Characteristic Pieces, Op.10

Edward Elgar

Rosemary

('That's For Remembrance', Douce Pensée)

Edward Elgar

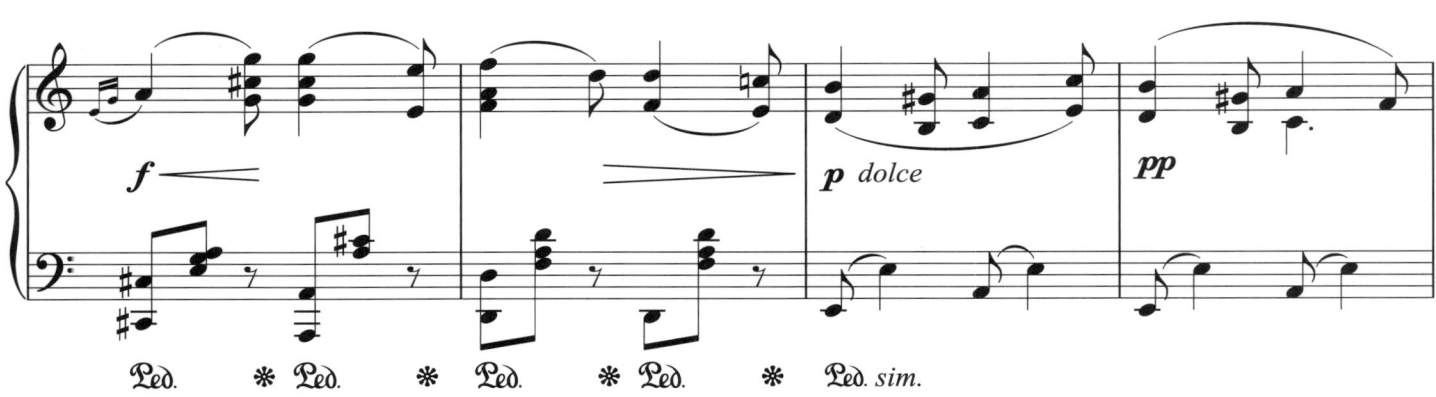

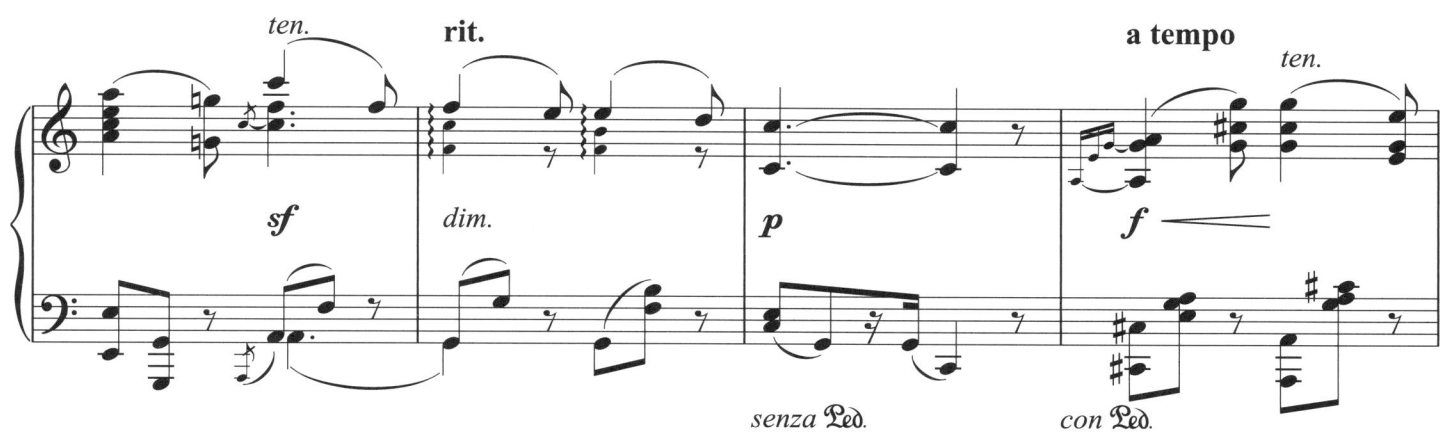

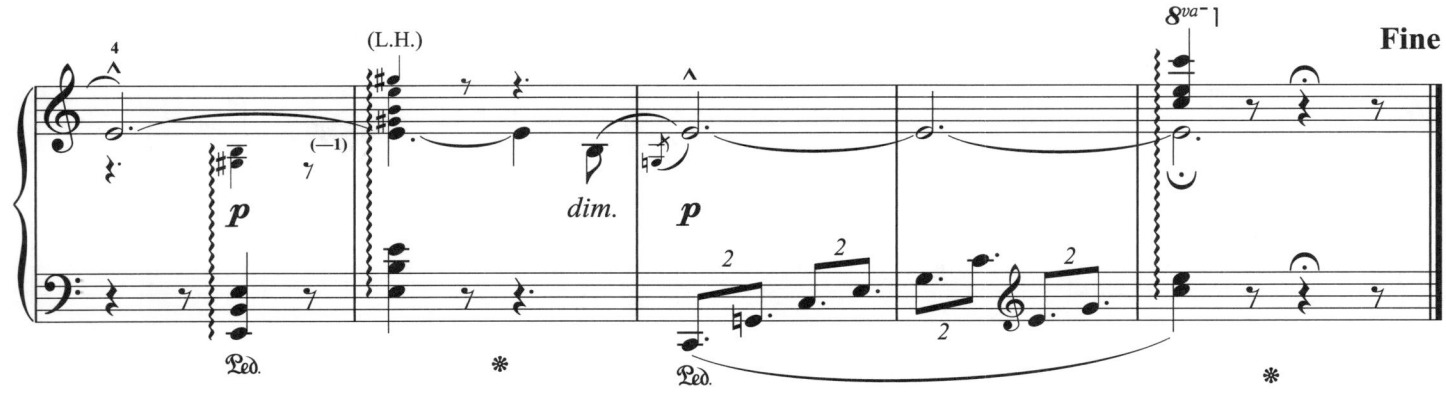

Sonatina

Edward Elgar

I.

48

II.

Allegro

Variations On An Original Theme (Enigma), Op.36

Edward Elgar

Theme

Variation 2: H.D.S-P.

Variation 8: W.N.

attacca
Var.9 'Nimrod'

Variation 9: Nimrod

Variation 13: ***

Variation 14 (Finale): E.D.U.

Where Corals Lie

No.4 *from* Sea Pictures, Op.37

Edward Elgar

74

Violin Concerto in B Minor, Op.61

(Opening)

Edward Elgar

largamente   A tempo

molto largamente